CHRISTIAN
BASICS
BIBLE
STUDIES

Excellence

RUN WITH THE HORSES

Eugene Peterson
with Scott Hotaling

6 STUDIES FOR INDIVIDUALS OR GROUPS
WITH LEADER'S NOTES

Inter-Varsity Press
Leicester, England

IVP Connect
An imprint of InterVarsity Press
Downers Grove, Illinois

InterVarsity Press, USA
P.O. Box 1400, Downers Grove, IL 60515-1426, USA
World Wide Web: www.ivpress.com
Email: email@ivpress.com

Inter-Varsity Press, England
Norton Street, Nottingham NG7 3HR, England
World Wide Web: www.ivpbooks.com
Email: ivp@ivpbooks.com

©1994 by Eugene Peterson

InterVarsity Press®, U.S.A., is the book-publishing division of InterVarsity Christian Fellowship/USA®, a movement of students and faculty active on campus at hundreds of universities, colleges and schools of nursing in the United States of America, and a member movement of the International Fellowship of Evangelical Students. For information about local and regional activities, write Public Relations Dept., InterVarsity Christian Fellowship/USA, 6400 Schroeder Rd., P.O. Box 7895, Madison, WI 53707-7895, or visit the IVCF website at <www.intervarsity.org>.

This study guide is based on and adapts material from Run with the Horses © 1983 by InterVarsity Christian Fellowship of the United States of America.

Inter-Varsity Press, England, is closely linked with the Universities and Colleges Christian Fellowship (formerly the Inter-Varsity Fellowship), a student movement linking Christian Unions in universities and colleges throughout the United Kingdom and the Republic of Ireland, and a member movement of the International Fellowship of Evangelical Students. For information about local and national activities write to UCCF, 38 De Montfort Street, Leicester LE1 7GP, email them at email@uccf.org.uk, or visit the UCCF website at www.uccf.org.uk.

Cover design: Cindy Kiple; cover photograph: Cheryl Ogilvie/iStockphoto

USA ISBN 978-0-8308-2011-5
UK ISBN 978-0-85111-377-7

Printed in the United States of America ∞

g **green**
press
INITIATIVE InterVarsity Press is committed to protecting the environment and to the responsible use of natural resources. As a member of the Green Press Initiative we use recycled paper whenever possible. To learn more about the Green Press Initiative, visit <www.greenpressinitiative.org>.

P   26   25   24   23   22   21   20   19   18   17   16

Y   26   25   24   23   22   21   20   19

CONTENTS

Christian Basics Bible Studies

Knowing Christ is where faith begins. From there we grow through the essentials of discipleship: Bible study, prayer, Christian community and much more. We learn to set godly priorities, grow in Christian character and witness to others. We persevere through doubts and grow in wisdom. These are the topics woven into each of the Christian Basics Bible Studies. Working through this series will help you become a more mature Christian.

WHAT KIND OF GUIDE IS THIS?

The studies are not designed to merely tell you what one person thinks. Instead, through inductive study, they will help you discover for yourself what Scripture is saying. Each study deals with a particular passage—rather than jumping around the Bible—so that you can really delve into the author's meaning in that context.

The studies ask three different kinds of questions. *Observation* questions help you to understand the content of the passage by asking about the basic facts: who, what, when, where and how. *Interpretation* questions delve into the meaning of the passage. *Application* questions help you discover its implications for growing in Christ.

These three keys unlock the treasures of the biblical writings and help you live them out.

This is a thought-provoking guide. Each question assumes a variety of answers. Many questions do not have "right" answers, particularly questions that aim at meaning or application. Instead, the questions should inspire users to explore the passage more thoroughly.

This study guide is flexible. You can use it for individual study, but it is also great for a variety of groups—student, professional, neighborhood or church groups. Each study takes about forty-five minutes in a group setting or thirty minutes in personal study.

How They're Put Together

Each study is composed of four sections: opening paragraphs and questions to help you get into the topic, the NIV text and questions that invite study of the passage, questions to help you apply what you have learned, and a suggestion for prayer.

The workbook format provides space for writing a response to each question. This format is ideal for personal study and allows group members to prepare in advance for the discussion and/or write down notes during the study. This space can form a permanent record of your thoughts and spiritual progress.

At the back of the guide are study notes that may be useful for leaders or for individuals. These notes do not give "the answers," but they do provide additional background information on certain questions to help you through the difficult spots. The "Guidelines for Leaders" section describes how to lead a group discussion, gives helpful tips on group dynamics and suggests ways to deal with problems that may arise during the discussion. With such helps, someone with little or no experience can lead an effective group study.

SUGGESTIONS FOR INDIVIDUAL STUDY

1. This guide is based on a classic book or booklet that will enrich your spiritual life. If you have not read the book or booklet suggested in the "Further Reading" section, you may want to read the portion suggested before you begin your study. The ideas in the book will enhance your study, but the Bible text will be the focus of each session.

2. Read the introduction. Consider the opening questions and note your responses.

3. Pray, asking God to speak to you from his Word about this particular topic.

4. Read the passage reproduced for you from the New International Version. You may wish to mark phrases that seem important. Note in the margin any questions that come to your mind as you read.

5. Use the questions from the study guide to more thoroughly examine the passage. Note your findings in the space provided. After you have made your own notes, read the corresponding study notes in the back of the book for further insights.

6. Reread the entire passage, making further notes about its general principles and about the way you intend to use them.

7. Move to the "Commit" section. Spend time prayerfully considering what the passage has to say specifically to your life.

8. Read the suggestion for prayer. Speak to God about insights you have gained. Tell him of any desires you have for specific growth. Ask him to help you as you attempt to live out the principles described in that passage.

SUGGESTIONS FOR MEMBERS OF A GROUP STUDY

Joining a Bible study group can be a great avenue to spiritual growth. Here are a few guidelines that will help you as you participate in the studies in this guide.

1. Reading the book suggested as further reading, before or after each session, will enhance your study and understanding of the themes in this guide.

2. These studies focus on a particular passage of Scripture—in depth. Only rarely should you refer to other portions of the Bible, and then only at the request of the leader. Of course, the Bible is internally consistent. Other good forms of study draw on that consistency, but inductive Bible study sticks with a single passage and works on it in depth.

3. These are discussion studies. Questions in this guide aim at helping a group discuss together a passage of Scripture in order to understand its content, meaning and implications. Most people are either natural talkers or natural listeners, yet this type of study works best if people participate more or less evenly. Try to curb any natural tendency to either excessive talking or excessive quiet. You and the rest of the group will benefit.

4. Most questions in this guide allow for a variety of answers. If you disagree with someone else's comment, gently say so. Then explain your own point of view from the passage before you.

5. Be willing to lead a discussion, if asked. Much of the preparation for leading has already been accomplished in the writing of this guide.

6. Respect the privacy of people in your group. Many people speak

of things within the context of a Bible study/prayer group that they do not want to be public knowledge. Assume that personal information spoken within the group setting is private, unless you are specifically told otherwise. And don't talk about it elsewhere.

7. We recommend that all groups follow a few basic guidelines and that these guidelines be read at the first session. The guidelines, which you may wish to adapt to your situation, are the following:

a. Anything said in this group is considered confidential and will not be discussed outside the group unless specific permission is given to do so.

b. We will provide time for each person present to talk if he or she feels comfortable doing so.

c. We will talk about ourselves and our own situations, avoiding conversation about other people.

d. We will listen attentively to each other.

e. We will pray for each other.

8. Enjoy your study. Prepare to grow.

SUGGESTIONS FOR GROUP LEADERS

There are specific suggestions to help you in leading in the "Guidelines for Leaders" and in the "Study Notes" at the back of this guide. Read the "Guidelines for Leaders" carefully, even if you are only leading one group meeting. Then you can go to the section on the particular session you will lead.

How Will You Compete with Horses?

The puzzle is why so many people live so badly. Not so wickedly, but so inanely. Not so cruelly, but so stupidly. There is little to admire and less to imitate in the people who are prominent in our culture. We have celebrities but not saints.

This condition has produced an odd phenomenon: individuals who live trivial lives and then engage in evil acts in order to establish significance for themselves. Assassins and hijackers attempt the gigantic leap from obscurity to fame by killing a prominent person or endangering the lives of an airplane full of passengers. Often they are successful. The mass media report their words and display their actions. Writers vie with one another in analyzing their motives and providing psychological profiles of them.

If, on the other hand, we look around for what it means to be a mature, whole, blessed person, we don't find much. These people are around, maybe as many of them as ever, but they aren't easy to pick out. No journalist interviews them. No talk show features them. They're not admired. They are not looked up to. They do not set trends. There is no cash value in them. No Oscars are given for integrity. At year's end no one compiles a list of the ten best-lived lives.

DULL VIRTUE?

In novels and poems and plays most of the memorable figures are either villains or victims. Good people, virtuous lives, mostly seem a bit dull. Jeremiah is a stunning exception. For most of my adult life he has attracted me. The complexity and intensity of his person caught and kept my attention. The captivating quality in the man is his goodness, his virtue, his excellence. He lived at his best. His was not a hothouse piety, for he lived through crushing storms of hostility and furies of bitter doubt. There is not a trace of smugness or complacency or naiveté in Jeremiah—every muscle in his body was stretched to the limits by fatigue, every thought in his mind subjected to rejection, every feeling in his heart put through fires of ridicule. Goodness in Jeremiah was not "being nice." It was something more like *prowess*.

There is a memorable passage concerning Jeremiah's life, when, worn down by the opposition and absorbed in self-pity, he was about to capitulate to an inner death. He was ready to abandon his unique calling in God and settle for being a Jerusalem statistic. At that critical moment he heard the reprimand: "If you have raced with men on foot, and they have worn you out, how will you compete with horses? If you stumble in safe country, how will you manage in the thickets by the Jordan?" (Jeremiah 12:5).

Life is difficult, Jeremiah. Are you going to quit at the first wave of opposition? Are you going to retreat when you find that there is more to life than finding three meals a day and a dry place to sleep at night? Are you going to run home the minute you find that the mass of men and women are more interested in keeping their feet warm than in living at risk to the glory of God? Are you going to live cautiously or courageously? I called you to live at your best, to pursue righteousness, to sustain a drive toward excellence.

It is easier to relax in the embracing arms of The Average. Easier, but not better. Easier, but not more significant. Easier, but not more fulfilling. I called you to a life of purpose far beyond what you think yourself capable of living, and I promised you adequate strength to fulfill your destiny. Now at the first sign of difficulty you are ready to quit. If you are fatigued by this run-of-the-mill crowd of apathetic mediocrities, what will you do when the real race starts, the race with the swift and determined horses of excellence? What is it you really want, Jeremiah? Do you want to shuffle along with this crowd or to run with the horses?

It is unlikely, I think, that Jeremiah was spontaneous or quick in his reply to God's question. The ecstatic ideals for a new life had been splattered with the world's cynicism. The euphoric impetus of youthful enthusiasm no longer carried him. He weighed the options. He counted the cost. He tossed and turned in hesitation. The response when it came was not verbal but biographical. His life became his answer: "I'll run with the horses."

For further reading: chapter one of Run with the Horses. *(This guide builds on ideas outlined in* Run with the Horses. *Recommended reading at the end of each study points you to the appropriate section of that book.)*

Pleading Inadequacy

Jeremiah 1:4-16

If we are asked to do something that we know we cannot do, it is foolish to accept the assignment, for it soon becomes an embarrassment to everyone. God asked Jeremiah to do something he couldn't do. Naturally, he refused. The job Jeremiah refused was to be a prophet.

No job is more important, for what is more important than a persuasive presentation of the invisible but living reality—God? And what is more important than a convincing demonstration of the eternal meaning of the visible, ordinary stuff of daily life? But more important or not, Jeremiah refused. He was not qualified. He had not done well in the God courses in school. And he hadn't been around long enough to know how the world works. " 'Ah, Sovereign LORD,' I said, 'I do not know how to speak; I am only a child' " (Jeremiah 1:6).

There is an enormous gap between what we think we can do and what God calls us to do. Our ideas of what we can do or want to do are trivial; God's ideas for us are grand. God's call to Jeremiah to be a prophet parallels his call to us to be a person. The excuses we make are plausible; often they are statements of fact, but they are excuses all the same and are disallowed by our Lord, who says: "Do not say,

'I am only a child.' You must go to everyone I send you to and say whatever I command you. Do not be afraid of them, for I am with you and will rescue you" (Jeremiah 1:7-8).

 OPEN

- Think of a time when someone asked you to do something you thought was over your head. What feelings did you have about attempting the task?

What reasons did you have to not try?

Did those reasons keep you from trying? Why or why not?

- What helps you feel encouraged when you have a difficult task set before you?

 STUDY

Read Jeremiah 1:4-16.
[4]The word of the LORD came to me, saying, [5]"Before I formed you

in the womb I knew you, before you were born I set you apart; I appointed you as a prophet to the nations."

⁶"Ah, Sovereign LORD," I said, "I do not know how to speak; I am only a child." ⁷But the LORD said to me, "Do not say, 'I am only a child.' You must go to everyone I send you to and say whatever I command you. ⁸Do not be afraid of them, for I am with you and will rescue you," declares the LORD.

⁹Then the LORD reached out his hand and touched my mouth and said to me, "Now, I have put my words in your mouth. ¹⁰See, today I appoint you over nations and kingdoms to uproot and tear down, to destroy and overthrow, to build and to plant."

¹¹The word of the LORD came to me: "What do you see, Jeremiah?"

"I see the branch of an almond tree," I replied.

¹²The LORD said to me, "You have seen correctly, for I am watching to see that my word is fulfilled."

¹³The word of the LORD came to me again: "What do you see?"

"I see a boiling pot, tilting away from the north," I answered.

¹⁴The LORD said to me, "From the north disaster will be poured out on all who live in the land. ¹⁵I am about to summon all the peoples of the northern kingdoms," declares the LORD. "Their kings will come and set up their thrones in the entrance of the gates of Jerusalem; they will come against all her surrounding walls and against all the towns of Judah. ¹⁶I will pronounce my judgments on my people because of their wickedness in forsaking me, in burning incense to other gods and in worshiping what their hands have made."

---

1. Summarize the dialogue between the Lord and Jeremiah in this chapter.

2. What is Jeremiah's initial reaction to God's call on his life (v. 6)?

---

3. How does God reassure Jeremiah that he is capable of being God's prophet (vv. 7-10)?

---

4. Jeremiah was "appointed" by God to be a prophet to the nations (v. 5). What has God "appointed" you to do or be? It might not seem as important as Jeremiah's call, but God does have a unique and original adventure for each of us. Here are some ideas:

- teaching Sunday school

- starting a Bible study at work

- providing a Christian example for your family

- praying for others

- campaigning for a local candidate you believe in

- witnessing to your neighbors

5. We too are good at pleading inadequacy in order to avoid living at the best God calls us to. How tired the excuses sound! "I am too young"; "I am only a layperson"; "I don't have time." What reasons do you use to resist God's call on your life?

6. God showed Jeremiah two visions in this dialogue (vv. 11-16). What is the significance of the vision in verses 11-12?

What is the significance of the vision in verses 13-16?

7. In verse 19 the Lord says, "They will fight against you but will not overcome you, for I am with you and will rescue you." In what ways has God communicated reassurance that he will help you to become the person you are called to be—even in the face of opposition?

8. Jeremiah lived in a changing and dangerous world, much like our own. How do you see God's hand controlling evil in the world?

 COMMIT

■ How can you be more open to both God's call and God's reassurance to you?

■ Make a list of people, experiences, Scripture passages or signs that remind you of God's presence in your life. Each day focus on one item on the list, thanking God for it.

Offer God your praise for his work in your life—in the past, present and future.

For further reading: *chapters two through four of* Run with the Horses.

Discernment

Jeremiah 7:1-15

Words are important—immensely important. What we say and the way we say it expresses what is most personal and intimate in us. But mindlessly repeating holy words no more creates a relationship than saying "I love you" twenty times a day makes us skilled lovers.

The outside is a lot easier to reform than the inside. Going to the right church and saying the right words is a lot easier than working out a life of justice and love among the people you work and live with. Showing up at church once a week and saying a hearty amen is a lot easier than engaging in a life of daily prayer and Scripture meditation, which develops into concern for poverty and injustice, hunger and war.

Are the people who do this deliberately trying to pull the wool over the eyes of their neighbors and fake God into blessing them? Some are, but for most I don't think so. I don't think they are trying to get by with anything. I think they have lived for so long on the basis of outward appearances that they have no feel for inward reality. We live in a culture where a new beginning is far more attractive than a long follow-through. Images are important. Beginnings are important. But an image without substance is a lie. A beginning without a continuation is a lie. This is the important message Jeremiah has for Israel.

OPEN

■ A camera commercial states, "Image is everything." How does our culture emphasize image over substance? (Consider movies, TV shows, music, politics.)

■ How do you think people perceive you?

■ When has someone's perception of you influenced your actions?

 STUDY

Read Jeremiah 7:1-15.

¹This is the word that came to Jeremiah from the LORD: ²"Stand at the gate of the LORD's house and there proclaim this message:

" 'Hear the word of the LORD, all you people of Judah who come through these gates to worship the LORD. ³This is what the LORD Almighty, the God of Israel, says: Reform your ways and your actions, and I will let you live in this place. ⁴Do not trust in deceptive words and say, "This is the temple of the LORD, the temple of the LORD, the temple of the LORD!" ⁵If you really change your ways and your actions and deal with each other justly, ⁶if you do not oppress the alien, the fatherless or the widow and do not shed innocent blood in this place, and if you do not follow other gods to your own harm, [7]then I will let you live in this place, in the land I gave your forefathers for ever and ever. [8]But look, you are trusting in deceptive words that are worthless.

[9]" 'Will you steal and murder, commit adultery and perjury, burn incense to Baal and follow other gods you have not known, [10]and then come and stand before me in this house, which bears my Name, and say, "We are safe"—safe to do all these detestable things? [11]Has this house, which bears my Name, become a den of robbers to you? But I have been watching! declares the LORD.

[12]" 'Go now to the place in Shiloh where I first made a dwelling for my Name, and see what I did to it because of the wickedness of my people Israel. [13]While you were doing all these things, declares the LORD, I spoke to you again and again, but you did not listen; I called you, but you did not answer. [14]Therefore, what I did to Shiloh I will now do to the house that bears my Name, the temple you trust in, the place I gave to you and your fathers. [15]I will thrust you from my presence, just as I did all your brothers, the people of Ephraim.' "

---

1. Describe the attitude of the Israelites as they approached worship.

---

2. What deceptive words were the Israelites trusting?

Why were they appealing?

---

3. In what ways might your church or fellowship be clinging to deceptive words?

---

4. In what ways did the Israelites need to change (vv. 6-9)?

---

5. What is the connection between worship and how we live our lives?

---

6. What are the consequences of obeying or disobeying God according to these verses (vv. 3, 7, 14-15)?

7. False prophets were deceiving the Israelites and keeping them from listening to God: "I spoke to you again and again, but you did not listen" (v. 13). What keeps you from hearing God's instructions?

COMMIT

■ People's lives are only as good as their worship. How has worship affected the way you live?

■ How do deceptive words (image) keep you from experiencing God in true worship (substance)?

■ To prepare for worship this week, ask God how you need to change your ways and actions (v. 5). Spend time in confession and listen for God's word of forgiveness and restoration.

Thank God for the privilege that he extends to us of coming to dwell in his house of worship.

For further reading: *chapter five of* Run with the Horses.

God's Shaping Hand
Jeremiah 18:1-18

Try to imagine how life would change if we had no containers in which to store anything; no pots and pans, no bowls and dishes, no buckets and jugs, no cans and barrels, no cardboard boxes and brown paper bags, no grain silos and oil storage tanks. Life would be reduced to what we could manage in a single day with what we could hold in our hands at one time. Pottery made it possible for communities to develop. Life was extended beyond the immediate, beyond the urgent.

There is something else that is just as important. No one has ever been able to make a clay pot that is *just* a clay pot. Every pot is also an art form. Pottery is always changing its shape as potters find new proportions, different ways to shape the pots in pleasing combinations of curves. There is no pottery that besides being useful does not also show evidence of beauty. Pottery is artistically shaped, designed, painted, glazed, fired. It is one of the most functional items in life; it is also one of the most beautiful.

We commonly separate the useful and the beautiful, the necessary and the elegant. We build featureless office buildings and ugly factories for our necessary work; then we build museums to contain the objects of beauty.

Each human being is an inseparable union of necessity and freedom. There is no human being who is not useful with a part to play in what God is doing. And there is no human being who is not unique with special lines and colors and forms distinct from anyone else.

All this became clear to Jeremiah in the potter's house: the brute fact of the clay—lumpish and inert—shaped for a purpose by the hands of the potter, and then, as it took shape, the realization of the uniquely designed individuality and wide-ranging usefulness it would acquire as a finished pot, painted and baked and glazed. God shapes us for his eternal purposes, and he begins right here. The dust out of which we are made and the image of God into which we are made are one and the same.

OPEN

- Think of a time when you had a plan to create something but you couldn't complete the project because you needed someone else who wasn't willing to help. What were your reactions, internal and external, to the other person?

- Now think of a time when your plan worked well because the other person was willing and eager to help. What were your reactions this time?

- When has a person who seemed ordinary on the outside served you in a way that was particularly meaningful?

 STUDY

Read Jeremiah 18:1-18.

¹This is the word that came to Jeremiah from the LORD: ²"Go down to the potter's house, and there I will give you my message." ³So I went down to the potter's house, and I saw him working at the wheel. ⁴But the pot he was shaping from the clay was marred in his hands; so the potter formed it into another pot, shaping it as seemed best to him.

⁵Then the word of the LORD came to me: ⁶"O house of Israel, can I not do with you as this potter does?" declares the LORD. "Like clay in the hand of the potter, so are you in my hand, O house of Israel. ⁷If at any time I announce that a nation or kingdom is to be uprooted, torn down and destroyed, ⁸and if that nation I warned repents of its evil, then I will relent and not inflict on it the disaster I had planned. ⁹And if at another time I announce that a nation or kingdom is to be built up and planted, ¹⁰and if it does evil in my sight and does not obey me, then I will reconsider the good I had intended to do for it.

¹¹"Now therefore say to the people of Judah and those living in Jerusalem, 'This is what the LORD says: Look! I am preparing a disaster for you and devising a plan against you. So turn from your evil ways, each one of you, and reform your ways and your actions.' ¹²But they will reply, 'It's no use. We will continue with our own plans; each of us will follow the stubbornness of his evil heart.' "

[13]Therefore this is what the LORD says: "Inquire among the nations: Who has ever heard anything like this? A most horrible thing has been done by Virgin Israel. [14]Does the snow of Lebanon ever vanish from its rocky slopes? Do its cool waters from distant sources ever cease to flow? [15]Yet my people have forgotten me; they burn incense to worthless idols, which made them stumble in their ways and in the ancient paths. They made them walk in bypaths and on roads not built up. [16]Their land will be laid waste, an object of lasting scorn; all who pass by will be appalled and will shake their heads. [17]Like a wind from the east, I will scatter them before their enemies; I will show them my back and not my face in the day of their disaster."

[18]They said, "Come, let's make plans against Jeremiah; for the teaching of the law by the priest will not be lost, nor will counsel from the wise, nor the word from the prophets. So come, let's attack him with our tongues and pay no attention to anything he says."

---

1. What words would you use to describe God's feelings about the nation of Israel in this passage?

---

2. What words could be used to describe Jeremiah's feelings?

---

3. What would be a contemporary parallel to the analogy of the

potter: someone who tries to create something but needs the participation of whatever is being molded?

4. In what ways did the nation of Israel resist being molded by God (vv. 13-15)?

5. What was God's response to their resistance (vv. 16-17)?

6. What are some of the ways that people today, especially Christians, resist being molded by God?

7. Jeremiah had to pay a price for allowing God to mold him. In fact he was repeatedly criticized, cursed, slandered and thrown into jail (v. 18). What price have you had to pay for following God in the past?

8. When has God showed patience with you, starting over in his effort to mold you?

9. Knowing that we all sometimes resist God's workings, why do you think God puts up with us?

COMMIT

■ What are some actions—however small—you can take to help God mold you into a more mature Christian?

■ What are some possible frustrations or hardships you might face by allowing God to mold you? Try to be specific.

Talk to God about the work he is doing and will be doing in you. Freely express your fear and hesitation as well as your excitement.

For further reading: *chapters six and seven of* Run with the Horses.

Honesty
Jeremiah 15:10-21

In the spring of 1980, Rosie Ruiz was the first woman to cross the finish line of the Boston Marathon. She had the laurel wreath placed on her head in a blaze of lights and cheering. She was completely unknown in the world of running. An incredible feat! Her first race a victory in the prestigious Boston Marathon!

Then someone noticed her legs—loose flesh, cellulite. Questions were asked. No one had seen her along the 26.2 mile course. The truth came out: she had jumped into the race during the last mile.

There was immediate and widespread interest in Rosie. Why would she do that when it was certain that she would be found out? Athletic performance cannot be faked. But she never admitted her fraud. She repeatedly said that she would run another marathon to validate her ability. Somehow she never did.

One interviewer concluded that she really believed she had run the complete Boston Marathon and won. She was analyzed as a sociopath. She lied convincingly and naturally with no sense of conscience, no sense of reality in terms of right and wrong, acceptable and unacceptable behavior. She appeared bright, normal and intelligent. But there was no moral sense to give coherence to her social actions.

In reading about Rosie I thought of all the people I know who want to get in on the finish but who cleverly arrange not to run the race.

They appear in church on Sunday wreathed in smiles, entering into the celebration, but there is no personal life that leads up to it or out from it. Occasionally they engage in spectacular acts of love and compassion in public. They are plausible and convincing. But in the end they do not run the race, believing through the tough times, praying through the lonely, angry, hurt hours. They have no sense for what is *real* in religion. The proper label for such a person is *religiopath*.

No one becomes human the way Jeremiah was human by posing in a posture of victory. It was his prayers, hidden but persistent, that brought him to the human wholeness and spiritual sensitivity that we want to emulate. What we do in secret determines the soundness of who we are in public.

 ## OPEN

■ Recall a time when you felt deserted by God. What were the circumstances that helped you to feel God's presence again?

■ Think of the three most memorable prayer experiences you have had. What did they all have in common?

 ## STUDY

Read Jeremiah 15:10-21.

[10]Alas, my mother, that you gave me birth, a man with whom the whole land strives and contends! I have neither lent nor borrowed, yet everyone curses me.

[11]The LORD said, "Surely I will deliver you for a good purpose; surely I will make your enemies plead with you in times of disaster and times of distress. [12]Can a man break iron—iron from the north—or bronze? [13]Your wealth and your treasures I will give as plunder, without charge, because of all your sins throughout your country. [14]I will enslave you to your enemies in a land you do not know, for my anger will kindle a fire that will burn against you."

[15]You understand, O LORD; remember me and care for me. Avenge me on my persecutors. You are long-suffering—do not take me away; think of how I suffer reproach for your sake. [16]When your words came, I ate them; they were my joy and my heart's delight, for I bear your name, O LORD God Almighty. [17]I never sat in the company of revelers, never made merry with them; I sat alone because your hand was on me and you had filled me with indignation. [18]Why is my pain unending and my wound grievous and incurable? Will you be to me like a deceptive brook, like a spring that fails?

[19]Therefore this is what the LORD says: "If you repent, I will restore you that you may serve me; if you utter worthy, not worthless, words, you will be my spokesman. Let this people turn to you, but you must not turn to them. [20]I will make you a wall to this people, a fortified wall of bronze; they will fight against you but will not overcome you, for I am with you to rescue and save you," declares the LORD. [21]"I will save you from the hands of the wicked and redeem you from the grasp of the cruel."

---

1. In this passage we get a glimpse of the inner life of Jeremiah and his relationship to his God. What does this passage tell you about the kind of person Jeremiah is?

2. What are Jeremiah's concerns in his prayer?

3. Jeremiah was extremely honest in his prayer to God. When do you find it difficult to be honest with God?

4. What do you think Jeremiah wants God to tell him?

5. What is God's response to Jeremiah's heartfelt prayer (vv. 19-21)?

6. Think of a time when God's response to your prayer was unexpected or surprising to you. What were the circumstances?

7. Jeremiah was God's prophet, who found himself alone in follow-

ing God's commands to a holy life. Why do you think God called Jeremiah to repentance in verse 19?

---

8. Most Christians go through periods when God's demands on their lives seem unreasonable or unfair. How do you strike a balance between feeling like a self-righteous martyr and realizing that God is always right?

 COMMIT

■ How can you be more honest with God, and yourself, when you pray?

■ Jeremiah must have been open to whatever God's response would be. Make it your goal to hear God's response to your prayers, and not just what you want to hear.

Begin the conversation with God by expressing the concerns that are on your mind today—even if they seem trivial or unreasonable. Be sure to allow time to listen for God's response.

For further reading: *chapter eight of* Run with the Horses.

Obedience

Jeremiah 35

The moral level of our society is shameful. The spiritual integrity of our culture is an embarrassment. Any part of our lives that is turned over to the crowd makes it and us worse. The larger the crowd, the smaller our lives. Pliny the Elder once said that the Romans, when they couldn't make a building beautiful, made it big. The practice continues to be popular: If we can't do it well, we make it larger. We add dollars to our incomes, rooms to our houses, activities to our schedules, appointments to our calendars. And the quality of our lives diminishes with each addition.

On the other hand, every time that we retrieve a part of our lives from the crowd and respond to God's call to us, we are that much more ourselves, more human. Every time we reject the habits of the crowd and practice the disciplines of faith, we become a little more alive. In this passage Jeremiah shows what obedience looks like when a group of people make a commitment to hear God's call.

 OPEN

- List various choices you make that put you in a majority or dominant group in our society. Some examples could be a favorite sports team, restaurant or television show.

■ Think of an individual or group that stands out from the crowd because they live by their own standards. What are their attractive qualities?

What keeps you from following their example?

 STUDY

Read Jeremiah 35.

[1]This is the word that came to Jeremiah from the LORD during the reign of Jehoiakim son of Josiah king of Judah: [2]"Go to the Recabite family and invite them to come to one of the side rooms of the house of the LORD and give them wine to drink."

[3]So I went to get Jaazaniah son of Jeremiah, the son of Habazziniah, and his brothers and all his sons—the whole family of the Recabites. [4]I brought them into the house of the LORD, into the room of the sons of Hanan son of Igdaliah the man of God. It was next to the room of the officials, which was over that of Maaseiah son of Shallum the doorkeeper. [5]Then I set bowls full of wine and some cups before the men of the Recabite family and said to them, "Drink some wine."

[6]But they replied, "We do not drink wine, because our forefather

Jonadab son of Recab gave us this command: 'Neither you nor your descendants must ever drink wine. [7]Also you must never build houses, sow seed or plant vineyards; you must never have any of these things, but must always live in tents. Then you will live a long time in the land where you are nomads.' [8]We have obeyed everything our forefather Jonadab son of Recab commanded us. Neither we nor our wives nor our sons and daughters have ever drunk wine [9]or built houses to live in or had vineyards, fields or crops. [10]We have lived in tents and have fully obeyed everything our forefather Jonadab commanded us. [11]But when Nebuchadnezzar king of Babylon invaded this land, we said, 'Come, we must go to Jerusalem to escape the Babylonian and Aramean armies.' So we have remained in Jerusalem."

[12]Then the word of the LORD came to Jeremiah, saying: [13]"This is what the LORD Almighty, the God of Israel, says: Go and tell the men of Judah and the people of Jerusalem, 'Will you not learn a lesson and obey my words?' declares the LORD. [14]Jonadab son of Recab ordered his sons not to drink wine and this command has been kept. To this day they do not drink wine, because they obey their forefather's command. But I have spoken to you again and again, yet you have not obeyed me. [15]Again and again I sent all my servants the prophets to you. They said, "Each of you must turn from your wicked ways and reform your actions; do not follow other gods to serve them. Then you will live in the land I have given to you and your fathers." But you have not paid attention or listened to me. [16]The descendants of Jonadab son of Recab have carried out the command their forefather gave them, but these people have not obeyed me.'

[17]"Therefore, this is what the LORD God Almighty, the God of Israel, says: 'Listen! I am going to bring on Judah and on everyone living in Jerusalem every disaster I pronounced against them. I spoke to them, but they did not listen; I called to them, but they did not answer.' "

¹⁸Then Jeremiah said to the family of the Recabites, "This is what the LORD Almighty, the God of Israel, says: 'You have obeyed the command of your forefather Jonadab and have followed all his instructions and have done everything he ordered.' ¹⁹Therefore, this is what the LORD Almighty, the God of Israel, says: 'Jonadab son of Recab will never fail to have a man to serve me.' "

---

1. What was unique about the Recabites (vv. 6-7)?

---

2. What did God tell Jeremiah to offer the Recabites?

What was the context of this offer?

---

3. What does their refusal tell you about the Recabites?

4. What parallel does Jeremiah draw between the standards of the Recabites and what God expected from the people of Jerusalem (vv. 12-16)?

5. How had the people responded to God's messages through the prophets?

6. In what areas of your life do you sense God calling you to higher standards than those who surround you?

7. What factors might have made it easier for the Recabites to keep the commands of their ancestors?

How can you include these factors in your life to help you remain faithful to God's calling on your life?

 COMMIT

- In verse 19 God makes a promise to the Recabites, based on their obedience, that they will always be allowed to serve him. How have you seen God give you opportunities to serve when you have been faithful to God's standards?

- List the choices you make that put you in the world's sphere of influence. How do these choices keep you from living up to God's standards?

Pray that God will give you the courage and conviction to overcome the factors in your life that keep you from following him.

For further reading: *chapters nine through eleven of* Run with the Horses.

Making the Best of It

Jeremiah 29:1-14

Daily we find ourselves in places we don't want to be with people we don't want to be with. We face decisions on how we will respond to these "exile" conditions. We can say: "I don't like it; I want to be where I was ten years ago. How can you expect me to throw myself into what I don't like—that would be sheer hypocrisy. What sense is there in taking risks and tiring myself out among people I don't even like in a place where I have no future?"

Or we can say: "I will do my best with what is here. Far more important than the climate of this place, the economics of this place, the neighbors in this place, is the God of this place. God is here with me. What I am experiencing right now is on ground that was created by him and with people whom he loves. It's just as possible to live out the will of God here as any place else. Change is hard. Building relationships in unfamiliar and hostile surroundings is difficult. But if that is what it means to be alive and human, I will do it."

François Fenelon used to say that there are two kinds of people: some look at life and complain of what is not there; others look at life and rejoice in what is there. Will we live on the basis of what we don't have or what we do have? This was Jeremiah's choice.

? OPEN

- Think about a time of change in some part of your life:

  __ relationships   __ work   __ where you live

  __ growing older   __ church   __ all of the above

- How has change caused you to lose your focus on what is important?

- What issues in your life seem to use up your energy or distract your attention?

- Most of us have a vision for how we think our lives should be arranged so that God can use us most effectively. What does your vision look like?

Study

Read Jeremiah 29:1-14.

¹This is the text of the letter that the prophet Jeremiah sent from Jerusalem to the surviving elders among the exiles and to the priests, the prophets and all the other people Nebuchadnezzar had carried into exile from Jerusalem to Babylon. ²(This was after King Jehoiachin and the queen mother, the court officials and the leaders of Judah and Jerusalem, the craftsmen and the artisans had gone into exile from Jerusalem.) ³He entrusted the letter to Elasah son of Shaphan and to Gemariah son of Hilkiah, whom Zedekiah king of Judah sent to King Nebuchadnezzar in Babylon. It said:

⁴This is what the LORD Almighty, the God of Israel, says to all those I carried into exile from Jerusalem to Babylon: ⁵"Build houses and settle down; plant gardens and eat what they produce. ⁶Marry and have sons and daughters; find wives for your sons and give your daughters in marriage, so that they too may have sons and daughters. Increase in number there; do not decrease. ⁷Also, seek the peace and prosperity of the city to which I have carried you into exile. Pray to the LORD for it, because if it prospers, you too will prosper." ⁸Yes, this is what the LORD Almighty, the God of Israel, says: "Do not let the prophets and diviners among you deceive you. Do not listen to the dreams you encourage them to have. ⁹They are prophesying lies to you in my name. I have not sent them," declares the LORD.

¹⁰This is what the LORD says: "When seventy years are completed for Babylon, I will come to you and fulfill my gracious promise to bring you back to this place. ¹¹For I know the plans I have for you," declares the LORD, "plans to prosper you and not to harm you, plans to give you hope and a future. ¹²Then you will call upon me and come and pray to me, and I will listen to you. ¹³You will seek me and find me when you seek me with all your heart. ¹⁴I will be found by you," de-

clares the LORD, "and will bring you back from captivity. I will gather
you from all the nations and places where I have banished you," declares the LORD, "and will bring you back to the place from which I
carried you into exile."

---

1. What is the situation into which Jeremiah sent his letter?

---

2. What were some of the changes the exiles had to learn to deal with?

---

3. What is the essence of Jeremiah's instructions in verses 4-9?

---

4. Why do you think Jeremiah found it necessary to give this message?

5. Think of a time when you felt like an exile in a strange country. What emotions and/or reactions did you experience?

How did your relationship with God change during that time?

6. Reread verses 10-14. What possible reactions would you expect from the exiles in Babylon when they heard these words?

7. What parallels do you see between the Jews who were exiled and your life as a Christian?

8. How do the words of verses 10-14 encourage you as you try to re-
    main faithful to God in a strange and change-filled society?

 COMMIT

■ Think of three ways that you can be more open to being used by
  God in the situation you find yourself in.

How will you act on them?

*Ask God to show you the gifts he offers you in the midst of the physical
place and time you are dwelling in. Thank him for the good gifts you
find in culture.*

For further reading: *chapters twelve through sixteen of* Run with the
Horses.

GUIDELINES FOR LEADERS

Leading a Bible discussion can be an enjoyable and rewarding experience. But it can also be intimidating—especially if you've never done it before. If this is how you feel, you're in good company.

Remember when God asked Moses to lead the Israelites out of Egypt? Moses replied, "O Lord, please send someone else to do it" (Ex 4:13). But God gave Moses the help (human and divine) he needed to be a strong leader.

Leading a Bible discussion is not difficult if you follow certain guidelines. You don't need to be an expert on the Bible or a trained teacher. The suggestions listed below can help you to effectively fulfill your role as leader—and enjoy doing it.

PREPARING FOR THE STUDY

1. As you study the passage ahead of time, ask God to help you understand it and apply it in your own life. Unless this happens, you will not be prepared to lead others. Pray too for the various members of the group. Ask God to open your hearts to the message of his Word and motivate you to action.

2. Read the introduction to the entire guide to get an overview of the subject at hand and the issues that will be explored.

3. Be ready for the "Open" questions with a personal story or example. The group will be only as vulnerable and open as its leader.

4. Read the chapter of the companion book that is suggested under "Further Reading" at the end of each study.

5. As you begin preparing for each study, read and reread the assigned Bible passage to familiarize yourself with it. You may want to look up the passage in a Bible so that you can see its context.

6. This study guide is based on the New International Version of the Bible. That is what is reproduced in your guide. It will help you and the group if you use this translation as the basis for your study and discussion.

7. Carefully work through each question in the study. Spend time in meditation and reflection as you consider how to respond.

8. Write your thoughts and responses in the space provided in the study guide. This will help you to express your understanding of the passage clearly.

9. It might help you to have a Bible dictionary handy. Use it to look up any unfamiliar words, names or places.

10. Take the final (application) questions and the "Commit" portion of each study seriously. Consider what this means for your life, what changes you may need to make in your lifestyle and/or what actions you can take in your church or with people you know. Remember that the group will follow your lead in responding to the studies.

LEADING THE STUDY

1. Be sure everyone in your group has a study guide and Bible. Encourage the group to prepare beforehand for each discussion by

reading the introduction to the guide and by working through the questions in the study.

2. At the beginning of your first time together, explain that these studies are meant to be discussions, not lectures. Encourage the members of the group to participate. However, do not put pressure on those who may be hesitant to speak during the first few sessions.

3. Begin the study on time. Open with prayer, asking God to help the group understand and apply the passage.

4. Have a group member read the introductory paragraph at the beginning of the discussion. This will remind the group of the topic of the study.

5. Every study begins with a section called "Open." These "approach" questions are meant to be asked before the passage is read. They are important for several reasons.

First, there is always a stiffness that needs to be overcome before people will begin to talk openly. A good question will break the ice.

Second, most people will have lots of different things going on in their minds (dinner, an exam, an important meeting coming up, how to get the car fixed) that have nothing to do with the study. A creative question will get their attention and draw them into the discussion.

Third, approach questions can reveal where our thoughts or feelings need to be transformed by Scripture. That is why it is especially important not to read the passage before the approach question is asked. The passage will tend to color the honest reactions people would otherwise give, because they feel they are supposed to think the way the Bible does.

6. Have a group member read aloud the passage to be studied.

7. As you ask the questions, keep in mind that they are designed to be used just as they are written. You may simply read them aloud. Or you may prefer to express them in your own words.

There may be times when it is appropriate to deviate from the study guide. For example, a question may already have been answered. If so, move on to the next question. Or someone may raise an important question not covered in the guide. Take time to discuss it, but try to keep the group from going off on tangents.

8. Avoid answering your own questions. Repeat or rephrase them if necessary until they are clearly understood. An eager group quickly becomes passive and silent if members think the leader will give all the *right* answers.

9. Don't be afraid of silence. People may need time to think about the question before formulating their answers.

10. Don't be content with just one answer. Ask, "What do the rest of you think?" or, "Anything else?" until several people have given answers to a question.

11. Acknowledge all contributions. Be affirming whenever possible. Never reject an answer. If it is clearly off-base, ask, "Which verse led you to that conclusion?" or, "What do the rest of you think?"

12. Don't expect every answer to be addressed to you, even though this will probably happen at first. As group members become more at ease, they will begin to truly interact with each other. This is one sign of healthy discussion.

13. Don't be afraid of controversy. It can be stimulating! If you don't resolve an issue completely, don't be frustrated. Move on and keep it in mind for later. A subsequent study may solve the problem.

14. Periodically summarize what the group has said about the passage. This helps to draw together the various ideas mentioned and gives continuity to the study. But don't preach.

15. Don't skip over the application questions at the end of each study. It's important that we each apply the message of the passage to ourselves in a specific way. Be willing to get things started by describing how you have been affected by the study.

    Depending on the makeup of your group and the length of time you've been together, you may or may not want to discuss the "Commit" section. If not, allow the group to read it and reflect on it silently. Encourage members to make specific commitments and to write them in their study guide. Ask them the following week how they did with their commitments.

16. Conclude your time together with conversational prayer. Ask for God's help in following through on the commitments you've made.

17. End on time.

Many more suggestions and helps are found in The Big Book on Small Groups *by Jeffrey Arnold.*

Study One.   PLEADING INADEQUACY. Jeremiah 1:4-16.

Purpose: To explore God's call to each of us and how we can respond positively.

Question 1.

Try to focus the discussion for this question on the flow of the dialogue, and avoid getting caught up in the specific meaning of the details.

Question 3.

God's reassurance to Jeremiah may not seem very comforting to us. God does not send us into the life of faith because we are qualified; he chooses us in order to qualify us for what he wants us to be and do. Yet God makes it clear to Jeremiah that, if Jeremiah lives up to his calling, God's presence will protect and sustain him.

Questions 4-5.

While few of us are called by God in the same way as Jeremiah, God does have a mission for each of us to be a part of. And like Jeremiah most of us have more than enough excuses ready. We offer excuses because we are convinced that we are plain and ordinary. The town or city that we live in, the neighborhood we grew up in, the friends we are stuck with—all seem undramatic. We see no way to be significant in such settings. Yet something very different takes place in the life of faith: each person discovers all the elements of a unique and original adventure. God's creative genius is endless. Each life is a fresh canvas on which he uses lines and colors, shades and lights, textures and proportions that he has never used before. It is as we participate in what God initiates in our lives that we find purpose.

Question 6.

Both of these visions may seem strange to us, but each communicated something deep and vital to Jeremiah. The almond tree is one of the earliest trees to bloom in Palestine. As a sign of spring, it is an anticipation, a promise of what is to come. There is also a word-play between the Hebrew words for *almond* and *watching*. God is promising Jeremiah that he will take care of Jeremiah and Jeremiah's message, and the almond branch becomes a visible reminder of that reassurance.

The boiling pot is partially explained in the passage. In the changing world order of Jeremiah's time the military threat was the Neo-Babylonian empire, which within a few years would attack Jerusalem. While this vision is negative, there are two implications which may have been comforting for Jeremiah: first, that the coming evil was under God's control, and second, that it did have limits.

Question 7.

Jeremiah's assurances seemed to come from God directly; most people are not so fortunate. So encourage others to think of people or events that God has used to speak to them. Often God's messages come through very subjective experiences. Other people may find reassuring signs in nature, like Jeremiah with the almond branch.

Question 8.

This is not an easy question, and group members may be intimidated by it. Give them time to think, and be ready to jump in with your own example. Group members will feel more comfortable if you take the lead in showing them that they can be vulnerable.

Study Two.   DISCERNMENT. Jeremiah 7:1-15.

Purpose: To learn to recognize the difference between image and substance.

Question 1.

Many of the Israelites evidently approached worship with a sense of complacency, stupidly pleased with themselves, putting their faith in the latest reform slogan.

Question 2.

False prophets were leading the people to believe that God's presence in Jerusalem, and especially in the temple, meant that God's power would always protect those within the city. Carried to its extreme, this meant that their actions had no affect on God's promised protection, despite Jeremiah's persistent preaching to the contrary.

Question 5.

Our lives are defined by our worship; by what we choose to worship, by the intensity and depth of our worship. Meaning and the importance of values become clear when our worship has integrity. When it does not, then our lives become shapeless and confused.

Study Three.   GOD'S SHAPING HAND. Jeremiah 18:1-18.

Purpose: To understand how God wants to shape us and how we participate in that process.

Open.

If no one in the group can think of a time when they had to create something, ask them to role-play or pretend that they have to create something together when not everyone is willing to help.

Question 1.

God's words to and through Jeremiah show a wide range of emotions. Although the most obvious emotions are "negative," note the tenderness in God's willingness to change his plans if Israel repents. (Note that in Jonah 3 God does indeed change his plan for the city of Nineveh.) God wanted to be merciful to Israel and, like the potter, try again to mold the people.

Question 2.

If members of the group are uncomfortable hypothesizing about Jeremiah's feelings, ask them to put themselves in his sandals and express what their feelings would be.

Question 3.

One example that might shed light on Jeremiah's analogy is the idea of a parent trying to mold a child into a mature person. This might help group members focus on the emotional investment God had in Israel.

Question 4.

For a more detailed list see Jeremiah 7:1-11. In short, the people of Israel had not lived up to their end of the covenant with God. The most obvious sign of this was their recurring worship of the false gods of their neighbors.

Question 6.

Our resistance to God may not be as obvious as Jeremiah's denunciation of Israel. However, many of us, even Christians, place goals, ideas or values above God's desires for us. It might also be good to try to identify some of the underlying reasons that people resist God's working. For example, one reason that the Israelites made idols was because they needed the reassurance of something concrete and physical, instead of trusting in an unseen God.

Question 7.

Also see Jeremiah 20. Few people in Western nations will face anything like Jeremiah's struggles. However, even in places where Christianity is "accepted," Christians face a choice between a religion which supports and reinforces cultural models of success or an encounter with the living God which may require going against popular ideas, values and choices. For those who choose the latter, anything (mockery, pain, renunciation, self-denial) will be accepted in order to deepen and extend the relationship with God.

Study Four.   **HONESTY. Jeremiah 15:10-21.**

Purpose: To discover how Jeremiah's life of prayer enabled him to be God's true servant.

Open.

When discussing the question about memorable prayer experiences, group members should look for elements that were common to all three experiences. For example, all three might have been during an emotionally difficult time, or when praying specifically for other people, or during a time of decision. Or perhaps the similarities are more general, such as a feeling of dependence on God, or a period of questioning God.

Question 1.

If there is confusion, it may be good to outline the dialogue of the passage. Verse 10 is Jeremiah speaking, rhetorically, to his mother. Verses 11-14 are God's response—Jeremiah will be delivered and his enemies defeated. Verses 15-18 are Jeremiah explicitly praying to God, and in 19-21 God responds again.

Question 2.

Jeremiah is really feeling sorry for himself. He is scared, lonely, hurt and angry. He feels that God's call on his life has robbed him of the comforts of being "normal." In the next chapter God will tell him not to marry and have children. He really feels as if he is an island. He was probably both attracted to the idea of being accepted by his fellow Israelites and repelled by their lifestyles. And deep down, he wanted to know that he was making a difference.

Question 4.

Jeremiah is in some sense desperate. Desperate to hear that things will turn out all right; desperate to know that God cares about him; desperate to know that God is really in control. But he also wants to hear that things are going to get easier, not harder.

Question 5.

Jeremiah's role in the prayer was to be honest with God and then to listen to God. God's role in the prayer was to restore and save Jeremiah. But he doesn't do it by giving easy answers. Instead, God feels Jeremiah's pain, but does not indulge it. God calls Jeremiah to repent and reestablish God's priorities in his life. As a result, God promises to renew Jeremiah.

Question 7.

Jeremiah needed to be reminded of what is important in life: loving his God and following his call. Jeremiah yearned, as we all do, for acceptance and an easier task; he had allowed the views of his neighbors to cloud his vision for what God had called him to do.

Question 8.

Many of us are tempted, like Jeremiah surely was, to compare our commitment and perseverance with what our society shows as acceptable or normal. When we do we are tricked into false feelings about how good and honorable we are. Instead, we need to realize that as Christians we are measured in comparison to our Lord, who not only asks the impossible of us, but gives us grace and his presence in our task.

Study Five.   **OBEDIENCE. Jeremiah 35.**

Purpose: To discover what it means to follow God obediently, and to discover the help that we can find as we serve God in community.

Open.

If the group has difficulty thinking of examples, you might mention the Amish or Mennonites, groups that refuse to adapt to many of the "conveniences" of modern life. Individuals that come to mind include Mother Teresa and Jimmy Carter, who use their status as celebrities to advocate issues of justice.

Question 1.

The Recabites were, in a sense, defined by what set them apart from the rest of Israelite society. In a society which increasingly depended on the stability of a central government and its alliances, the Recabites must have seemed to be a people of uncommon simplicity and faith. We know very little about them. In fact, this passage is the only time they are mentioned in the Bible. Several theories exist to explain their lifestyle. Two common theories are that they were either throwbacks to a simpler, more religious form of Israel, or that they were in the military-defense business and needed mobility and a strong sense of unity.

Question 2.

Not only does Jeremiah ask the Recabites to go against their vows, but he does so in the temple, in a public place, where they would have been seen by both God and other people.

Question 4.

God's expectations for his people often seemed strange when compared to the surrounding nations, who worshiped various gods of nature. They also no doubt seemed arbitrary and silly to those who forgot the context of the covenant, just as the way of life of the Recabites must have seemed strange and unnecessary to those who didn't understand it.

Question 7.

Regardless of why they followed their way of life, we can safely assume that the Recabites had several things going for them. They had a shared heritage, which gave them a strong sense of identity. They also appeared to have a strong sense of unity. And, naturally, it is often easier to live up to a standard when those around you are also trying to do so.

Study Six.   MAKING THE BEST OF IT. Jeremiah 29:1-14.

Purpose: To find courage to live as Christians in the midst of a hostile culture.

Question 1.

The basic scenario is seen in verses 1-3. However, more information can be implied from later in the chapter. Three false prophets—Ahab, Zedekiah and Shemiah—told the people what they wanted to hear: "Hang on a little longer and we'll get back. It can't be much longer." They even claimed their words came from God.

Question 3.

The exiles had listened to the lies of the false prophets. They wanted to believe that they would soon return to Jerusalem, and everything would be okay again. So they had no need to develop relationships, or care about Babylon at all. Jeremiah's letter was a reminder to them that God was not going to rescue them immediately, and that they needed to get on with their lives.

Christian Basics are the keys to becoming a mature disciple. The studies in these guides, based on material from some well-loved books (which can be read along with the studies), will take you through key Scripture passages and help you to apply biblical truths to your life. Each guide has six studies for individuals or groups.

CERTAINTY: *Know Why You Believe* by Paul Little. Faith means facing hard questions. Is Jesus the only way to God? Why does God allow suffering and evil? These questions need solid answers. These studies will guide you to Scripture to find a reasonable response to the toughest challenges you face.

CHARACTER: *Who You Are When No One's Looking* by Bill Hybels. Courage. Discipline. Vision. Endurance. Compassion. Self-sacrifice. The qualities covered in this Bible study guide provide a foundation for character. With this foundation and God's guidance, we can maintain character even when we face temptations and troubles.

CHRIST: *Basic Christianity* by John Stott. God himself is seeking us through his Son, Jesus Christ. But who is this Jesus? These studies explore the person and character of the man who has altered the face of history. Discover him for the first time or in a new and deeper way.

COMMITMENT: *My Heart—Christ's Home* by Robert Boyd Munger. What would it be like to have Christ come into the home of our hearts? Moving from the living room to the study to the recreation room with him, we discover what he desires for us. These studies will take you through six rooms of your heart. You will be stretched and enriched by your personal meetings with Christ in each study.

DECISIONS: *Finding God's Will* by J. I. Packer. Facing a big decision? From job changes to marriage to buying a house, this guide will give you the biblical grounding you need to discover what God has in store for you.

EXCELLENCE: *Run with the Horses* by Eugene Peterson. Life is difficult. Daily we must choose whether to live cautiously or courageously. God calls us to live at our best, to pursue righteousness, to sustain a drive toward excellence. These studies on Jeremiah's pursuit of excellence with God's help will motivate and inspire you.

HOPE: *Never Beyond Hope* by J. I. Packer and Carolyn Nystrom. Ever feel like a hopeless sinner? Look at the lives of Samson, Peter, Martha and more. The Bible was given to us to offer hope and encouragement through the testimonies of those that have gone before us. Through this guide, you'll discover that just as biblical characters failed, biblical characters were redeemed. And God wants to do the same for you.

PERSEVERANCE: *A Long Obedience in the Same Direction* by Eugene Peterson. When the going gets tough, what does a Christian do? This world is no friend to grace. God has given us some resources, however. As we grow in character qualities like hope, patience, repentance and joy, we will grow in our ability to persevere. The biblical passages in these studies offer encouragement to continue in the path Christ has set forth for us.

PRAYER: *Too Busy Not to Pray* by Bill Hybels. There's so much going on—work, church, school, family, relationships: the list is never-ending. Someone always seems to need something from us. But time for God, time to pray, seems impossible to find. These studies are designed to help you slow down and listen to God so that you can respond to him.

PRIORITIES: *Tyranny of the Urgent* by Charles Hummel. Have you ever wished for a thirty-hour day? Every week we leave a trail of unfinished tasks. Unanswered letters, unvisited friends and unread books haunt our waking moments. We desperately need relief. This guide is designed to help you put your life back in order by discovering what is *really* important. Find out what God's priorities are for you.

TRANSFORMATION: *Developing a Heart for God* by Rebecca Manley Pippert. Would you like to move from despair to hope? Would you like to transform your feelings of fear to faith? Would you like to turn envy into compassion? The Bible shows us how David turned these negative emotions in his life into godly character qualities. By studying his life and choices we can make the same transformation in our own lives.

WISDOM: *Making Life Work* by Bill Hybels. Some people spend their lives relying on the abundance of information that's out there. But sometimes knowledge isn't enough. When we're stuck and don't know where to turn for answers, Proverbs offers practical advice and spiritual wisdom for real-life questions so that we might become people who think and act out of godly wisdom.

WITNESSING: *How to Give Away Your Faith* by Paul Little. If you want to talk about Jesus, but you're not sure what to say—or how to say it—this Bible study guide is for you. It will deepen your understanding of the essentials of faith and strengthen your confidence as you talk with others.